BOBBY RIGGS'

ASPEN HUSTLE
Based on a true story

Marv Huss

Huss Publishing
P.O. Box 206
La Jolla, CA 92038
www.sallyhuss.com
ISBN 13:978-0-9822625-0-4

PROLOGUE

Flushing Meadows, New York
U.S. Open Championship 2007

    Newswire – Roger Federer from Basel, Switzerland, in a tightly contested Open final match against Novak Djokavic from Croatia, who upset second seed Rafael Nadal, won his 4th straight U.S. Open today and his 13th Grand Slam title. After the match Pete Sampras told a reporter, "No question in my mind, Roger is the best athlete in the world." It is very interesting that Pete didn't say that Roger was the best tennis player. He said, "Best athlete." That covers a lot of great folks in my mind. It has to include Tiger Woods, Pele, Michael Jordan, Peyton Manning, Shaq, Kelly Slater, Alex Rodriguez and tons more. Roger now only needs two more Grand Slams to break Pete Sampras' all-time Grand Slam record of 14. It took Sampras 12 years to set that record. Federer will have surpassed it in 5 years at the rate he's going. What he has done in the last 3 years is remarkable – and that's an understatement! In July of 2003 he won his first Grand Slam title – Wimbledon. That started a run of excellence he carries on to this day. Since then he has claimed 11 more Grand Slam events and held the top ranking in his sport with a relentless grip. And he's just getting started. His close friend Tiger Woods heartily agrees with Sampras that he is one of the best athletes in the world. "You bet he is!" says Tiger with a smile.

La Jolla, California
The La Jolla Beach and Tennis Club
Monday, noon

The La Jolla Beach and Tennis Club has played a large part in our family's life over the years. My wife Sally, our son Mike and I used to live up the street until we forsook the beauty of the ocean for the lure of the golf courses in the desert. The Club was our home away from home – to play a little tennis, visit with friends, walk the beach or have a glass of wine on the promenade, hoping to see a green flash at the sun's setting. Developed by a true patron of tennis and tennis players William S. Kellogg, the Club was transformed from its original marina design into a hacienda style resort right on the sand. It sprawls along the beach front, quietly welcoming generations of families who come each summer for their vacations. And during the quiet months it remains its humble self, filled with locals who play on its 16 courts and who still sit on the promenade after a set or two, hoping to see a green flash. The green flash occurs on rare occasions when the sun hits the horizon at the end of a very clear day.

The Beach and Tennis Club is not the grandest

of all resorts in the world, but it has a certain some-thing that many of the newer and bigger operations do not possess. Perhaps, it's soul. It is probably the soul of the Kellogg family that continues to oversea the property. It could be the eons of paint that cover the adobe walls resulting in a color you can't quite identify. Is it salmon? Is it orange? Is it tan? The rooms are small, but are continually being upgraded. The grounds are kept immaculate with an infinite variety of palm trees swaying in the sea breeze high above the court fences. And there are roses, lots and lots of roses. Nothing significant has changed at the Club for years and probably that's what makes it so special. My wife can attest to that. She started playing here as a young girl in junior tournaments, then in women's events and finally in national senior championships, winning titles along the way. She is just one of the many champions who have played at the Club through the years. Stoffen, Mako, Budge, Gonzales, Kramer, Bond, Ralston, Olmedo, Bundy-Cheney, Fleitz, Brough, Laver, Emerson, Smith, Lutz, Rameriz, Edberg, Osuna, Pasarel, Roddick, Conners, Segura and a million more.

So it is with great excitement that we have returned to the La Jolla area, correcting the mistake of having left in the first place, and especially on this day returning to the Club to lunch with old friends.

Old friends are not just old, as in this case, but old as in good friends for a long time. Jay Paul the most vociferous of the luncheon attendees greets us with his usual enthusiasm, "Marv, Sally, great to see you. Roger was fantastic yesterday, wasn't he?! The greatest player I've ever seen!" Jay speaks with some authority, a former teaching pro out of Los Angeles, a connoisseur of tennis for many years, a heady competitor himself and now a scratch golfer. "He has everything," continues Jay. "His serve may not be as big as Roddick's, Pete's or Pancho's, but he's consistent and his placement is superb." His wife Sheri nods. She lets Jay do most of the talking most of the time. She sits quietly and waits her turn, usually when things quiet down. Learning the game in later life, Sheri herself has become a keen observer of the game.

"Uh huh," agrees Sheri.

"I'd have to agree too," adds Mardi Diller, another of our table companions. She has played social tennis at the Club for years and like Sheri, what she lacks in skill she makes up for in dress. These two are perhaps the best dressed players this side of Sharapova.

Mardi's husband Shell, who is usually as quiet as Sheri, breaks in, "I believe there are 8 critical skills to tennis greatness." Shell is a fine player and tough competitor. He is intelligent and mindful on and off the court so his opinion counts here. "Most champions possess 3 or 4 of these abilities in spades – a big serve, killer forehand, lethal backhand, aggressive volley, fantastic return, great court coverage, concentration and the ability to win critical points. I think Federer has them all. He is the greatest by default."

"I wouldn't disagree," says a voice from behind me. I turn to see that Jack and Carmen Scull have arrived to join the luncheon party. "He is the best I've ever seen," continues Jack, and Jack has seen a lot of tennis players over the years. He has been a member of the Club for 50 years and still plays a respectable game of doubles. His wife Carmen still turns heads when she enters a room. Her beauty is not just skin deep. She is lovely in every way and shares an interest with Sally in matters of a spiritual nature.

Sally chips in, "He plays in the ethers."

"What? What are you talking about?" demands Jay.

Sally has a tendency to see things in a different light, even if she is agreeing with everyone, as she was here. "Don't you see the way he moves around the court? He is absolutely one with the ball. He moves on a different plane, like Michael Jordan did on the basketball court. He is fluid. He is liquid. He is airborne. He is the greatest tennis player of all time. No one comes close!"

Words began to fly, but finally I couldn't take it anymore. "I strongly disagree!" I volunteered. The table conversation stopped. I continued, "I believe the greatest player is the one who has made the greatest impact on tennis to date and that was Bobby Riggs!"

"Riggs?!" yelled Jay. "He was a hustler. What did he ever do? What have I missed here?"

Now I had to explain myself. Diners at nearby tables were perking up their ears as our discussion became more heated. "First of all he was great – a world champion at the age of 21. He won the singles title at Wimbledon, 3 U.S. titles, played on the Davis Cup Team. He also won Wimbledon doubles and mixed doubles titles. He loved tennis and he too had all the shots and some trick ones not seen today. Yes, he was a hustler, but he was also a tennis promoter. In fact the single biggest tennis event, actually the single biggest athletic event, in history was created by Riggs. The Battle of the Sexes $100,000 Winner-Take-All match against Billie Jean King in 1973, up-lifted the awareness of tennis to the level of a major sport. There were 30,000, standing-room only at the Houston Astrodome with another 50 million TV viewers around the world. His efforts along with Billie Jean King's did more for women's lib than all the efforts up to that time. That event helped women break the equal pay and equal everything barrier in many, many fields beyond tennis. Besides all that he was a man in his mid-50's who could still play at a very high level. Sally and I know this from personal experience because he came to Aspen in 1976 to help us open a fabulous new tennis club called The Aspen Club."
Aspen, Colorado
Summer, 1975

Back in the mid 70's when Sally and I first got

together she was ending her career as a touring Virginia Slims tennis pro, still ranked in the top 20 in the world, and I had just left a top marketing and promotional position with Hallmark Cards in Kansas City to pursue my entrepreneurial destiny. We were offered a chance to go to Aspen with a deed to 25 spectacular acres of land along the Roaring Fork River, just south of town, to develop a world-class tennis resort for a New York investor. The deal was worked out on a paper napkin as we had lunch at the center court restaurant on the grounds of the old Forest Hills Tennis Club where the U.S. Open was being held. Sally would be the head rackets pro and I would supervise construction of the new club and the sale of 20 luxury condominiums scheduled to be built on the club property.

After Sally played her last Slims tournament in Austin, Texas, we packed our bags and headed for Aspen. The investor had wisely hired a local Aspen attorney, Andy Stern, for us to work with to secure the necessary local government approvals before starting construction on the project, as well as build an interest in the club for local and non-resident memberships. We would also have the 20 condos to sell.

So it was with great anticipation and a sense of freedom that we made our way by car along Interstate 70 out of Denver through the lower reaches of the Rockies toward our future.

We hit Glenwood Springs, then turned south on Highway 82 for the last 40 miles up along a narrow alpine valley bordering the Roaring Fork River. Cascading water ran from the higher elevations of Independence Pass and the Continental Divide into the river and down the valley. The fresh air and the possibility of wandering trout streams felt good to my soul. The aspen trees with their shimmering golden leaves welcomed us along our new path. "Sally, I know I'm going to like this project. I know it!"

As we passed through Carbondale, still climbing, the ranches looked grander, the cattle looked bigger and the river looked clearer. Finally at an altitude of 7,500 feet we entered the little town of Basalt, where yet another whitewater river roared. This one, running east to west, called the Frying Pan, falls into the Roaring Fork which runs south to north. The biggest landmark in Basalt is an old cowboy bar called the Frying Pan Restaurant and Bar. Right out of the 1800's, it is a hangout for after work ranch hands. "Let's stop," I said, eyeing some fishermen laying their catch out on the porch of the restaurant. I've got to check this out."

We climbed the steps and peeked into the creels the men brought to carry their catches. "Looks like you've had a good day," I ventured.

"Always a good day here. Always a good day," was the response from an old weather-beaten local still casting into the Frying Pan near the porch. But better still was the response from the restaurant. Wafting out of the doorway was the smell of fresh, pan-fried trout. The fisherman, who looked as if he had been in these mountains since birth, continued to fill me in, "Rainbows. We mostly catch rainbows with an occasional brownie here and there from the deep pools near the waterfall. But, if you're adventurous you can try a few high mountain lakes where you might catch some golden trout – above 10,000 feet. Great eatin'."

My mouth was watering, not only from the smells escaping from the nearby kitchen, but from the possibility of wandering stream and lake banks and actually catching fish. The most precious times in my youth were spent with my father doing just that – hopping from rock to rock, casting, reeling in, moving along and casting again with the promise of a fish dinner in the evening and all the while not paying attention to how my feet got me from one rock to the next.

"Could you give us a little background to this area? I asked. "Tell us about Aspen."

That brought a smile to the old man's face. His hands continued doing the tasks of a fisherman without his thinking about it. "Well, it goes back to the Ute Indians. For hundreds of years they used to summer in the high meadows here, hunting elk. In the late 1800's silver was discovered and all hell broke loose as miners came and raided the place. A large mining camp on the Roaring Fork developed called Ute City. It's now Aspen, but even then it had everything – an opera house, hotels, banks. Actually they're still here today – the Hotel Jerome, the Wheeler

Opera House, even the Ute City Bank. But like many good things, the boom didn't last. The price of silver crashed and the population which was nearly 12,000 dwindled to 800 people." He stopped to cast again.

"In the 30's, I believe it was, a wealthy Chicago industrialist named Walter Paepcke tried to build a ski resort, but World War II changed things. The area was turned into a training ground for the 10th Mountain Division to get our troops ready to fight the Germans in the alpine areas of Europe. That was my unit and after the war a bunch of us returned here. We loved it and knew it was special. Some of the men, like me, became ranchers. Others like Friedl Pfeifer formed the Aspen Ski Corp. That's how Aspen came to be."

We thanked our new friend and went inside to see if the trout tasted as good as it smelled.

The canyon narrows the last few miles into Aspen, winding above the river, then opens up into the last high meadow before climbing almost straight up to Independent Pass, the top of the Rocky Mountains with an altitude of over 12,000 feet. On that last high meadow sits the town of Aspen, now a sophisticated, refurbished Victorian village with its own airport capable of handling small private and corporate jets. Meticulously restored, the town glows from the faces of its charming multi-storied buildings and brick chalets with their arched windows and peaked roofs. The Aspen Music Festival was in full session when we arrived, with hundreds of student, classical musicians inhabiting every nook. Every street corner and every open window above every store along Galena, Hyman and Main streets was enlivened with their magical music making. They rehearsed 24/7 to the delight of the locals and their instructors who included many of the world's greatest musicians such as Izak Perlman.

Above the rooftops and the din, stood the most majestic of all mountains, Aspen Mountain, called Ajax by the locals. It soared from the center of town up through the clouds to 11,000 feet. This was indeed a sublime place and no wonder so many free-spirited celebrities like John Denver, Jack Nicholson, the Kennedys, Clint Eastwood and Merv Griffin made Aspen a regular stop or a second home.

So in the summer of 1975 we moved into an old sod-roofed ranch house in the middle of those 25 acres with the Roaring Fork River rumbling nearby. For the next year we worked hard and long to bring the proposed project to fruition. But it was when we got near the end of the construction phase that we decided that we needed a dramatic event to launch the membership program and to start the condominium sales.

We had it all. Our new mountainside complex boasted three indoor tennis courts, 12 outdoor courts, two squash courts, 16 racquetball courts, a full indoor gymnasium, an indoor swimming pool and spa, plus a beautiful restaurant, lounge and bar. On top of this, it was staffed by top health practitioners. Although there were five other tennis clubs in town, there was nothing like this in Aspen at the time. But we needed a big event to not only draw attention to the project, but also to draw attention to Sally, the first female head pro of a major tennis club in the U.S.

At a special breakfast meeting with our Aspen attorney, Andy, our New York investor, Ben Goldstein, and a few key Aspen local leaders, we proposed bringing Bobby Riggs to Aspen to play Sally in a winner-take-all exhibition tennis match. This was just 3 years after Bobby had played and beaten Margaret Court in a "Battle of the Sexes" match, claiming that no professional woman player, no matter how strong could beat a professional man player, no matter what his ranking. He proved it once. Then, of course, a few months later with that same bravado he took on Billie Jean King. Over 50,000,000 people worldwide watched that eventful match on TV. Bobby was featured on the cover of Time magazine. History was made as the glass ceiling of a cement tennis court was broken, thanks to Billie Jean.

We felt we could draw the attention we wanted with the help of Bobby. Fortunately, he was available. The deal we worked out was simple. It guaranteed him $3,500, plus a chance to win the $1,000 winner-take-all challenge money. Naturally we had to include his airfare, room and board, but that was easy. We were a resort. We also asked that he make himself available for socializing with our locals. He was only too willing. We planned to invite everybody in town to enjoy the event and the particular glam that he brought with him. Having never met Bobby Riggs, I really did not know what to expect, so we tried hard to cover all VIP treatment bases.

One of the key supporters of our project was the president of the local branch of a statewide bank chain. He suggested that their bank chain co-sponsor the event, not only to defray our costs, but as an incentive to their customers. They ended up giving away tickets at all of their branches throughout Colorado, for any new deposits of several thousand dollars or more.

Coloradans love any excuse to visit Aspen, so the event would not only bring potential new members to our club, but fill hotels, restaurants and the club stands. It would be a great promotion for everyone involved. The event was starting to grow and grow, taking on a life of its own. Again, I had never met Bobby Riggs, so I didn't know what to expect. But, this event was starting to ramp up – big time!

THE STORY

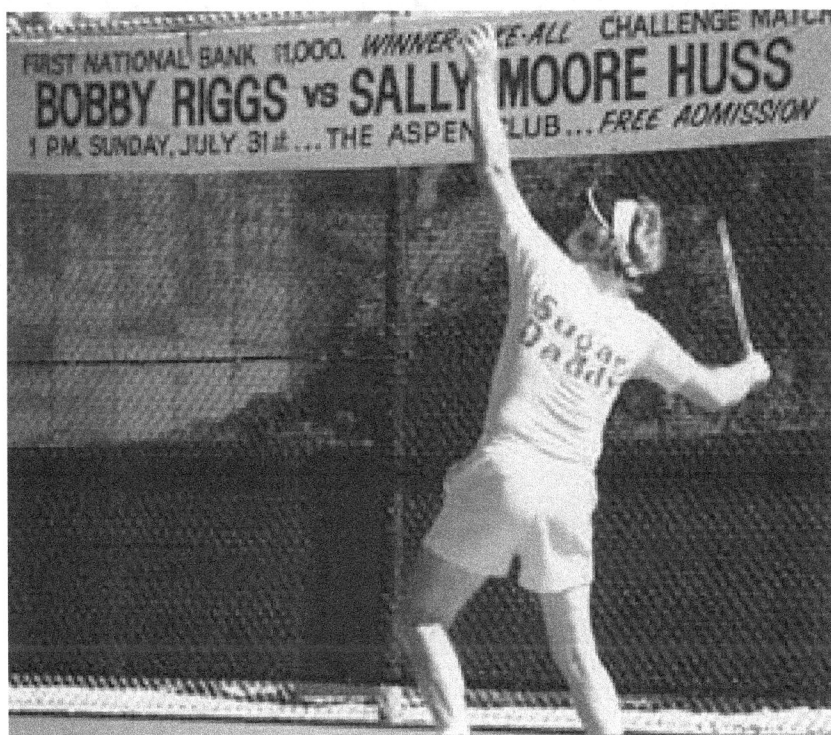

Aspen, Colorado
2:30 p.m., Wednesday, July 27, 1977
Aspen Airport

    I was to meet Bobby Riggs' Aspen Airways flight due in at 2:30 p.m. Aspen Airways was a small connector airline from Denver to Aspen. With only a 7,500 foot runway and at 8,000 feet altitude, only small corporate and private aircraft were permitted to land there. Aspen Airways flew small, twin-engine turbo prop puddle jumpers in and out continuously or as continuous as the weather would allow. On

15

stormy days they usually circled above the mountain peaks until they found a hole in the clouds, and then decended rapidly, spiraling down to the field. It was usually a traumatic event for newcomers, but commonplace to locals. Even on a clear day the mountain air could create a bumpy ride.

Fortunately today was a bright and sunny summer one, not a cloud, just a gentle breeze down the runway. It would probably be a mildly bumpy landing for the passangers. As the little commercial flight touches down and approaches the terminal where it will unload the passangers, I walk out onto the tarmac to greet the Man. Several young and happy couples come out first, then a rather smallish, discheveled mid-fifty-year-old man, who looks more like an old hippy than a legendary tennis icon, appears in the doorway. He seems a bit wobbly and is helped down the stairs by a fairly good-sized, good-looking, buxom, thirty-something woman. He is wearing a bright yellow Sugar Daddy. T-shirt Perhaps it is a one-size fits all, but it is two sizes too small. A potbelly pops out where his belt should be. I was stunned. This was my big event?

"Mr. Riggs, I'm Marv Huss from the Aspen Club. We're so honored to have you here," I sucked it up, hoping my disappointment was not evident. "I hope the flight didn't completely do you in. It's quite beautiful flying through the Rockies but they can be a little rough at times."

"Nice to be here," He says, holding out his

hand. "This is Nurse Nancy. She looks after me. We've been looking forward to this trip. We've never been to Aspen before. Thanks for inviting me. We'll have lots of fun." Fun! My God, this could be a fiasco!!

"Nancy has some concerns about my playing at this altitude at my age, but I'm sure that with a few days to get acclimated before Sunday, I'll be fine." Nurse Nancy smiles.

This is not at all what I expected. My heart sinks further when he adds fuel to my fears, "You know I played a small exhibition in L.A. last week and my elbow is still sore. Perhaps you could provide me with the name of a good doctor where I could get a cortizone shot."

"Of course, Bobby." So this was to be my "Great Event" to open the Club. My stomach churned. How could a man fall into such disrepair in such a short time? It was only a couple of years since he was at the top of his senior tennis game against Billie Jean.

My, oh, my! This is how the Third Battle of the Sexes began.

3:30 p.m., Wednesday, July 27
Town of Aspen

Aspen Airport is about four miles north of town and as we drive through Aspen I try to displace my concerns by giving Bobby and Nurse Nancy a little history lesson.

"Aspen was an old silver mining town in the 1800's and many of the buildings are the original buildings, but they have been meticulously restored to their charming Victorian state. I've accomodations for you in our best condo at the Aspen Club, overlooking the Roaring Fork River. But we will be dining each evening with some of the most influential people here, to kind of build the excitement for Sunday's match." Bobby doesn't look too happy about this. I babble on, "That's the old Wheeler Opera House...the Hotel Jerome...the Red Onion... the Ute City Bank...It's not really a bank, but a fine restaurant...This town has only 3,000 permanent residences now, but in the 1880's it was a great deal grander. It was wild miners and honkytonks. We're going to hit several of these spots, a different one each evening, with a different group, if you are up to it." I wasn't sure he was up to anything, but I didn't want to give him an out so I plowed on, "Everyone in town can't wait to meet you. The First National Bank is co-sponsoring the event and has folks coming in from all over the state to watch the match. Many are already here so the town is buzzing."

Just then we pass under one the street banners used to promote the event: "Bobby Riggs vs. Sally Moore Huss, Sunday July 31st in a Battle of the Sexes". "Nice touch, Marv," says Bobby, smiling graciously as he rubbed his elbow. I could see he was checking it all out. Nurse Nancy sat in the backseat, here to give any support he needed, I suppose.

"The Aspen Club is on the south side of town leading up to Independence Pass and the Continental Divide at 12,000 feet," I'd say anything to keep my mind off of my troubles.

Several turns later we entered the leichenstone gates of the new Aspen Club with our beautiful logo in bronze announcing its name above an aspen leaf, all embedded in wood. Trees to the right. Mirror Lake to the left and the Roaring Fork behind.

"Here we are. A three bedroom luxury unit that's never been slept in yet. It looks out to the Club across the river and has a nice spa and sauna in the master bath. I'd like to pick you up around 6 to join our mayor and the event planners for cocktails and dinner at the famed Crystal Palace. It's a landmark and the best Aspen has to offer. Everyone is dying to meet you."

"Marv, if I could beg off on this first night. I would really appreciate it. I could really use the rest." Nurse Nancy nods in agreement.

I felt at this point the match on Sunday was a wash and any mileage I could get out of our investment would have to be had before the event. I didn't want to tax the guy, but I had people lined up. "I really hate to ask you to do this, Bobby, but even if you could just make a brief appearance with this group it would get things off to a good start. They're our key supporters. I'll get you back as soon as I can."

"OK, but I may not last long. I really feel pretty weak. By the way, here's an envelope. I would like you to handle this. It's a few dollars that I would like to bet on the side. Even money, if any one thinks Sally can beat me."

Geeze, I hated to take the man's money. It was obvious he was struggling to just make an appearance, let alone win a tennis match. I was totally confused. Now I've become a bookie!

"One more thing, Marv, could you find me a warm-up partner to hit with around 9? I really need to see how this altitude is going to affect me, and see how my arm feels. Don't forget the doctor. Don't worry by Sunday, I'll be fine!"

Don't worry?! That's all I could do.

4:30 p.m., Wednesday, July 27
Attorney Andy Stern's office

Andy's law office was housed on the second floor of a beautiful old restored Victorian building overlooking Main Street. Bookcases full of law books and dark leather furniture filled the space. A Tiffany lamp or two added to the casual elegance. Andy, a very dapper Jerry Seinfield type in his mid-thirties and son of a former Czechslovakian Davis Cup player was a fine player himself and was eager for our project to succeed. He has been instrumental in the whole development of The Aspen Club, wrangling through city council agendas and legal matters of all shapes and sizes. He was a bright star in Aspen and I had turned to him whenever darkness crossed our path. Today I needed some light.

I slide into the leather couch in front of his desk and let out a deep sigh, "Well, I picked him up and dropped him at the Club condo. Frankly, I'm very concerned that he is going to be able to perform for us. He looks overweight, out of shape and sickly. He can hardly breathe at this altitude or hold a tennis racket because of a sore elbow. He needs rest, a cortizone shot and a bookie! He gave me this envelope of money to cover any side bets if anyone thinks Sally can actually beat him. I don't quite know what to do about all of it. I can't be his bookie, too!"

"Marv, relax, give me the envelope, I'll take care of it. Let's see what's in it."

Andy slices open the envelope and lets the contents spill across his desk. He shakes his head in disbelief. One hundred hundred dollar bills, $10,000 in all. Then he smiles and so do I.

"Marv, this is remakable. This 58 year-old man coming up here in this altitude, thinking he can beat Sally! Who did she play in the last couple of weeks? Yeah, every male pro in town and she beat them all. With her heavy groundstrokes and big serve, he doesn't have a chance. What is she, a couple of years older than Billie Jean? But she's in great shape. She'll be a big hero. Some of our locals will enjoy taking his money. Let me handle this. He'll get his $3,500 appearance money, plus a chance at the carrot of $1,000 prize money. What a dea!"

It is a small price to pay, if he is presentable. It's the 'if' that makes me uncomfortable. "Andy, he's asked me to get him a hitting partner each day to get used to the altitude. I think you should be the one. That way we'll know exactly what to expect. We may have to get Sally to lighten up on him on Sunday."

"Good idea." I feel a little better as I leave Andy's office.

5:30 p.m. Wednesday, July 27
Our sod-roofed ranch house

Sally is getting herself ready for the evening when I arrive. I want to share my concerns, yet I don't want to alarm her. She is fairly sensitive. "Hi, Honey. He's finally here. I think you might actually have to carry him to make the match interesting. He's in pretty bad shape physically. I'm a little worried that he can play well enough to give the spectators their money's worth – even if the event is free! Everybody in Colorado knows about this thing and thousands are coming in for it."

"Don't worry, Honey," she says, smiling brightly. "It'll be fun!"

'Worry' and 'fun', in my mind are mutually exclusive and I definitely cannot rid myself of the 'worry'. So 'fun' is out of the question. I'm the one who got this whole thing started, invested the money in bleachers and advertising, and even talked my buddy at the bank into co-sponsoring the event.

"He even tried to duck out of the first social event with the mayor tonight, but then agreed to make a brief appearance."

"It'll be fun," says Sally again. Sally was always into fun, but I didn't need a flop to open the Club.

7:00pm, Wednesday, July 27
Crystal Palace

The Crystal Palace dates back to the silver mining heydays of Aspen. It is one of the original two-story brick buildings that is a work of restorative art inside. To honor its name it has large crystal chandeliers bouncing light everywhere. There are Long, narrow dining tables, a big stage for follies-type entertainment and great cuisine. We have invited all the local dignitaries to be the first to meet the great Bobby Riggs.

The Palace is jammed this night as it is every night. Word spreads as we enter that the man is here. Everyone stands and applaudes. Bobby is charming, stops to chat or sign autographs as we make our way to our reserved table. It is hard to believe that an old-time tennis player could garner such admiration, but he created his real fame in his moment of glory as he went down in flames to Billie Jean King. He played the part of the likeable buffoon then. What kind of a part is he playing now? I'm thinking, "Alright! This is a good start!"

11:00 a.m. , Thursday, July28
Manager's Office, The Aspen Club

The phone rings in my office. My secretary Julie answers and indicates it is for me.

"Hey, Andy, how did the hit with Bobby go? What's the verdict?" My anxiety had still not subsided.

"Marv, you were right. He could only hit for 20 minutes and had to sit down. He's short of breath. He doesn't run very well and he was spraying the ball everywhere. He couldn't even handle my pace. It was a real struggle to keep a rally going. He apologized profusely and said his nurse was going to take him to see the doctor to get some relief for his elbow. He just wanted to take it easy the rest of the day. I agree with you that we might have a problem with him making a decent showing. He's got to get a whole lot better by Sunday. I'm hitting with him again tomorrow. Let's see if he improves. He did say that he and Nancy will be at our dinner tonight at the Ute City Bank. I'll see you there." That was it. My fears were confirmed. The event might really be a disaster. So we had to do the best we could with the people we were entertaining each evening to make sure they liked us and liked what we were doing as far as the Club was concerned.

7:00 p.m., Thursday, July28
Ute City Bank

The Ute City Bank still looks like the old silver mining depository of yesteryear on the outside, but like the Crystal Palace, the inside has been beautifully restored into a fine restaurant, including a vault for a wine cellar. The streets outside are full of tourists and many of them here for the big match. As we pull up to the restaurant the crowd spots Bobby and they start shouting, "Bobby! Bobby! Bobby!" and as he disembarks the van he is mobbed. Everyone wants to talk to him, kid him about being a chauvinist pig, find out why he lost to Billie Jean or how he was going to beat Sally. Inside the restaurant, he receives the same attention, a standing ovation, and some catcalls from the women in the room.

At the table he is seated next to Sally. It is the first time they have met. His eyes twinkle behind his glasses and his smile denotes a twinkle within, "So you're my date for Sunday! I've heard a lot about you, Sally, from your old coach at the L.A. Tennis Club, George Toley. And too from Billie Jean. She said she was 15 when you won the U.S. and Wimbledon Juniors. You were her idol. The number one Junior player in the world, then a semi-finalist the next year at Wimbledon, barely losing to the Brazilian Maria Bueno. Now, I hear you just beat the number four player on the Slims Tour, Wendy Overton. Well done. Well done. I'm very impressed, Sally. We should

25

have a lot of fun!

Sally smiles sweetly, maintaining her poise. She was cautious in receiving his compliments.

The mayor slides into the seat next to Bobby on the other side and they engage in a conversation about golf. Andy and I sit opposite him and watch the proceedings with great interest. Andy leans over to me and whispers, "Marv, you'll be happy to know that 5 different supporters of Sally have already covered half of Bobby's money. We should have it all down by Friday. They see it as easy money. Gotta think they're right. If I were a gambling man, I'd take a piece of it myself."

Bobby leans forward and asks me, "Marv, Mayor Stevens here has asked if you don't have anything for me Friday afternoon some of his friends would like me to join them for nine holes of golf over at Snowmass. He says the drives fly long at this altitude, 300 yards or more. This I'd like to see. Might help me get acclimated a little faster too."

"Sure, Bobby, just don't hurt yourself. You're our main attraction."

"No problem, Marv. One other thing I meant to mention to you last night. I would be happy to put on a tennis doubles exhibition for you Saturday to help build interest for Sunday. Maybe a couple of one-setters, with anyone you want. You'd be my partner to even things out. Maybe to make it interesting each player could put up $250. Winner-take-all. I'll cover you. Could be fun. Everyone wants to say they took money off of me. Might even fill the stands on Saturday, a bonus event. What do you say?"

I was a decent enough player, but his chances of winning with me as a partner against the better players in town had to be slim. Why am I worried again? He has only been here two days and it could cost him his appearance money and his own bankroll. I don't understand him. But I loved the idea!

9:00 p.m., Thursday, July 28
Our ranch house

"I'm not sure what to think of this guy," I tell Sally, as we return home. "For a semi-sick, worn-out old man, he still certainly draws a crowd. Andy told me that it's his understanding that the mayor's golf friends are high-rollers from Vegas. That doesn't make me feel too comfortable. Like flies to honey. Regardless, the town is humming and our event is really ramping up. I'm very pumped about that part."

Sally smiles a knowing smile, "Marv, don't underestimate him. I've known of his hustles for years -- playing with a frying pan or an ashtray instead of a racket. Playing left-handed. Tying a chair to his leg and when the bet was on, he could still beat the guy. He's legendary for these antics at the L.A. Tennis Club. No matter what his condition, he's still a very fine tennis player. I'm going into this like he's a really tough opponent and it's a really tough match. Don't get me involved with him anymore than necessary until after the match, please.!"

11:00 a.m., Friday, July 29
Gretel's on Ajax Mountain

Andy and I usually meet for strudel and coffee every Friday. To get to Gretel's you have to take the chair-lift up Ajax in the summer. During the winter we would always go up on the first chair-lift of the day to the top and ski down, breaking the new snow and stopping half-way at Gretel's mountain chalet for some of her famous, tasty pastry. Here we would recap the Aspen Club building progress for the week. That was the life of a businessman in Aspen. Today was different.

"Well Andy, did you hit with him again this morning? Has he recovered from his flight and last night's activities? Is he hitting any better?"

"Marv, I would say that he's a little more acclimated. He's hitting the ball a little stronger, but way below anything that will give Sally a real match. But I think he'll look good enough for the crowd. He's still not able to handle my pace, but he'll be able to go two sets, definitely not three." I feel a sense of relief. Then he continues, "Right as we were finishing our warm-up, the mayor and his Vegas friends showed up. They took him over to Snowmass for some golf. Looks like "fresh meat" for the sharks to me. Obviously he's feeling better.

28

He didn't beg off. By the way I've got some good news. Tom from the bank reports that we are going to have a full house on Sunday. The branches throughout the state report over 1,000 new savings accounts already. At $5000 each, that's over $5,000,000. You can bet the bank's very happy and we have 2000 ticket holders on-the-way. Not bad. Not bad at all! They're coming from Denver, Colorado Springs, even as far away as Fort Collins. Congratulations, Marv. The event is already a huge success. Stop worrying!"

I still just shake my head. Bad news! Good news! What's next?

7:00 p.m., Friday, July 29
Red Onion Restaurant

Sally and I lead Bobby and Nancy, through the jammed streets and into the over-crowded restaurant. The Red Onion is another restored relic from the 1800's. It is not as classy as the Crystal Palace, but a big favorite among the locals. During the ski season you need to make a reservation a season in advance or you can't even buy your way in during your stay. Bobby seems in great spirits. Perhaps the action on the golf course did him some good. I give Sally a squeeze and decide I'm finally going to enjoy the evening. Bobby is his ever gracious self, chit-chatting with everyone, shaking hands with the jocks and kissing cheeks of the ladies. Nurse Nancy keeps her eye on him, not allowing him to roam too far from her side. More than a nurse we could not say, but she is far too pretty to only be handing out pills with her bedside manner. Just like Nancy, the crowds love him.

Our guests tonight are business owners from the hotels, restaurants, sporting good stores, high-end jewelry and clothing boutiques. All of them were benefiting immensely from Bobby's visit. I sit across from Bobby, but Sally chooses to sit as far away as possible. As the fawning activity settles down, I lean over to Bobby and ask, "How did the golfing go today?"

"Marv, the two guys with the mayor were real hustlers. The mayor's a nice guy, but where did those two come from? They were serious golfers and serious gamblers."

Gad, I thought, more bad news, "What happened?"

"Well, in just nine holes, I lost $1,500. I really didn't have a chance. Not only was I not feeling great, but the ball at this altitude doesn't do what I think it's going to do. Now, they've got me committed again Saturday after our doubles exhibition. I've got to try and get my money back. At this rate I may lose all of the money I'll win by beating beat Sally. I'm not feeling too good right now. I would really like to cut out early tonight and go back to the condo and rest up. I'm going to need a miracle for tomorrow! Tell Andy that the doubles will be enough warm-up for me, so I don't need him until Sunday about 10:00 a.m. OK?"

10:00 a.m., Saturday, July 30
Aspen Club Tennis Stadium

I'm really pumped now. Thanks to Bobby's generosity, this extra event, the doubles exhibition, has brought out 2,500 fans to watch some of Aspen's top men tennis players play doubles against Bobby. When I went into my office at the Club my secretary informed me that we have had hundreds of resident and non-resident membership applications for the Club and that people are swarming through the new condos. There might be a couple of sales already. We're cooking. The event has really touched the pulse of the town. The atmosphere is just electric. If Sally can string him along to make a match out of it, we'll get some national press from this. It's really taken on a life of it's own, thanks to Bobby! No matter what happens now we will be huge winners!

As Bobby and I walk down to the court I try to tell him how much I appreciate what he has accomplished in a few short days. But he just smiles and says, "Let's just have fun, OK?" As we walk onto the court the fans all stand and cheer, "Bobby, Bobby, Bobby!" I found myself cheering too.

While I start hitting with our two opponents, both fine club players and much better than I, Bobby works the crowd – walking the entire first row of the length of the stadium, shaking hands and signing autographs. Then he greets our opponents and goes back to the base line and gently hits a few practice groundstrokes. "Hey, I'm ready. Let's play!"

The play began. Naturally our opponents tried to hit as many balls to me as possible, but if Bobby could reach a ball he would hit some off-speed shot, a junker, to set up a weak return and then he'd put it away. At five games all he stopped the match and asked our opponents, "I know you guys are going to beat us because we are really struggling here. But just to make it interesting Marv and I want to press the bet and make it $500 at corner. How does that sound?"

Without hesitation, they both smiled and agreed. They were clearly out playing me, but I hung in and the points got longer. The more I could stay in the point, the longer it got. The crowd loved it. Point after point I hung in just long enough for Bobby to get his racket on the ball and do something spectacular. My heart was pounding. Then after some wild points, Bobby ends up putting away a high lob and we took the set 8-6. Our opponents were dumbstruck. I was thrilled, even though I had not won a thing.

We sat on the side of the court, our opponents opened their billfolds and peeled off $500 each and handed the money to Bobby. By the look on their faces you knew they felt that this had been money well spent. One of them added his special appreciation,

"Thanks, Bobby. Wait till we tell our grandkids!"

The second match was almost the same, except they were even stronger players and quickly had us down 2-5, within one game of losing, again Bobby stopped the match and wanted to press the bet to $500 for each corner. Our opponents smiled and gave a 'thumbs up'. The crowd went wild. They were in on it. To my amazement Bobby kicked up his efforts a notch. His racket wizardry and court savvy were extraordinary from drop shots to topspin lobs he used it all. We won the match 7-5. All I could think was that Sally was going to have her hands full. There would be no walkover here.

After the match Bobby waved to the crowd. The mayor and his buddies were waiting with a car ready to whisk him away for a round of golf. I just shook my head in disbelief. He had just pocketed $2,000. The losers were happy to have played a tennis legend. He was definitely stronger, maybe too strong.

7:00 p.m., Saturday, July 31
Hotel Jerome

The town is bustling. Shops are full, restaurants full, bars full, streets crowded, people everywhere. Banners announcing the 'Battle of the Sexes' cross the main streets. Posters are in every window. Everybody was looking for Bobby Riggs. I've never seen any celebrity buzz quite like this and over one wizened up little, old man.

Sally and I were already in the Terrace Dining Room sitting with Andy. I was having a hard time controlling my enthusiasm. Friends and strangers were stopping by our table to express their pleasure in the happenings and wishing Sally well in her match tomorrow. Bobby was running a little late because of the golf game, but a roar from the crowd let us know he had arrived. He's laughing, glad-handing everyone as he makes his way through the crowd to our table. I remark to Andy, "I'll bet he got his money back from the sharks."

Overhearing my remark, Bobby tells a different tale, "Don't I wish. Those friends of the mayor's are not that friendly. I'm into them for $3,000. Can't wait for tomorrow. I really need the money!"

As sad as he speaks of his money woes, he puts on a different face to the crowd of well-wishers. He is the life of the party. Everyone wants meet him, greet him and to bet him – anything. He bets one man $100 that the next person to walk through the door at the hotel will be a woman. And most certainly it was!

Off to the side Andy lets me know, "We've got most of his money covered. Only a thousand dollars left. Sally's still a sure bet."

I felt she was too. "I'll take it. Put me down for the $1,000," I said. I too was caught up in the moment. A rush of adrenalin had passed through me and I could see the finish line ahead – the Club brimming with new members, condos all sold, everyone in town happy we were there and Sally floating to net shaking Bobby's weary hand and collecting the prize money.

"Well, Andy, call me in the morning after your hit with Bobby. He was playing some crafty tennis today, but then again Sally's something else!"

11:00 a.m., Sunday, July 31
Manager's Office, The Aspen Club

The big day has finally arrived. Andy walks into my office sweating profusely and slumps down in a chair. "Marv, we've got a problem. Rather Sally's got a problem."

"What's the problem? Is it his elbow? Has he pulled a muscle? What?!" I had to know. Things were going so well. At least so well until I told Sally that I had bet on her. She was a free spirit and had to play freely.   She had played for money on the Slims Tour, of course, but now she would be playing to not lose money. Definitely not a gambler. So, I already had a problem. I didn't need more.

"Well, he's hitting the ball not only on the lines, but I can't handle his pace. I can't stay with him. He's able to hit every shot in the book – drop shots, topspin lobs right on the baseline, slices that die, loopers that float and junk, all kinds of junk. He's not the same man. I'm thirty five and he wore me out in just 30 minutes. She's going to have her hands full today. But the crowd should love it."

1:00 p.m., Sunday, July 31
The Aspen Club
Center Court

It's a three-ringed circus-carnival atmosphere and all created by Bobby Riggs. He walks onto the court amid the roar of the fans. It's more like a rowdy bullfight crowd than a group of sedated tennis fans. "Bobby! Bobby!" they shout. He is decked out in his yellow Sugar Daddy, T-shirt, but now his pot belly is gone. He carries a sack of Sugar Daddy suckers and hands them out to the audience as he walks along the front row of the stands all the way around the court. He even gives one to the chair umpire and one to Sally. They meet at the net to decide by the flip of a coin who will serve first.

Sally looks fit and lovely in a new Michelle Palmer outfit, scarf around her head. But, I can see she's uneasy and not feeling steady. I hope once they start she will forget everything and play.

The match begins. The first few games are made up of long rallies, back and forth, up and back, nothing dramatic, just solid tennis. The crowd is appreciative and roars with every point Sally wins. She's a hometown gal now and has been touted as the favorite. She goes ahead 4-2 and looks in command of the match. Some of those who have bet on her yell the loudest. I'm included. As the match goes into the seventh game it is like a horse race when the horses turn for home. I look over to Andy and nod, what do you think? He shrugs, could go either way.

At 4-all Andy frowns. His face says it all. Look out, he's ratcheting up. Sally's got her hands full now! Doesn't look good. Sure enough he pulls ahead and wins the first set 6-4. Now Sally looks over at me as if to say this is the real Bobby Riggs! I give her a warm smile for she and I know this is exactly what I had hoped for – the perfect "Grand Opening" event – one that is going to put the Aspen Club on the map of this little town.

The second set starts with Bobby kicking into high gear. There is no question he is an artisan. He wields his racquet like a paintbrush on a grand canvas, mixing shots, pace and angles at will. He smoothly glides and slides around the court, pulling Sally as if on a tether. Then at just the right moment he opts for a soft drop shot. The crowd goes wild. Sally shows a little fatigue and soon it is 5-2 and match point. The crowd is mesmerized. They would like to see a third set, but it is not to be. The absolute last shot of the match finds Bobby at mid-court after a long rally. He winds up as if to hit a wedge shot out of a sand trap. Sending the ball straight up, then arching over the net, landing well in front of Sally and then with such reverse spin returning back over the net to Bobby without her even touching it. It was right out of the Harlem Globtrotters bag of tricks.

There was dead silence. Even Sally couldn't believe what she had seen. Then the crowd erupted in cheers.

We all knew we had just witnessed one of the world's greatest tennis players demonstrate, even in his late 50's and at 8,000 feet why he had won Wimbledon and the U.S. Open. Probably because he was known first and foremost as a hustler he would never receive the recognition he deserved. But on that day in Aspen the crowd knew, I knew it and Sally knew it.

Bobby made a sweeping gesture to the crowd, ran up to the net, gave Sally a big hug and a kiss, then quick as a wink headed for the mayor's car in the parking lot. As he passed me he said, "Marv, I really need your help. One last favor, please. Nancy has us all packed, but the mayor's boys are into me for some serious money and I promised them one more shot before I leave. I have a flight at 5:00 p.m. If you could have the van at the 18th green by 4:30 p.m. with the motor running, I think w can make it. Can you do that for me?"

I just shook my head, unbelievable. "Bobby, whatever you need. I'll be there for you. You did an extraordinary job for us. Thank you so much."

Andy grabs Bobby's arm before he gets in the car and hands him a very fat envelope. They shake hands and Bobby jumps in the car along side the mayor's cohorts, both eyeing the envelope.

4:30 p.m., Sunday, July 31
Snowmass Golf Club

Nurse Nancy and I drive through the parking lot at Snowmass over to the 18th green, near the clubhouse. I get out and walk to the edge of the green, checking my watch. Sure enough a foursome was just preparing to hit up on the green. Suddenly four balls land in rapid succession, plop, plop, plop, plop. Bobby's was the closest to the pin, but still some 20 feet away. No one spoke. Nobody was kibitzing. The match was obviously not over. I was wondering what was riding on it. The mayor and his friends putt out. Bobby stands over his 20 footer, then backs off to realign the putt. He stands over the ball again and again he backs off. Finally he stands over it and smoothly strokes the ball, dead center into the cup! Like the last point of the tennis match, you could hear a pin drop.

"Well, guys, like I told you I've got a 5:00 o'clock flight to catch. Gotta run."

One by one, the mayor included, each player steps up and begins peeling off $100 bills into Bobby's hands. I don't know how many, but a lot. Then he quicksteps into the van, shouting over his shoulder, "Hey guys, it's been fun. I hope we can do this again sometime -- soon! Thanks again Mr. Mayor."
They wave. We leave.

I don't know how much he won on the golf course, but now knowing what he was capable of he must have pressed the bet and pressed the bet and pressed the bet. His pockets were stuffed when he left, but we all got our money's worth in the end.

"Marv, let's get out of here quick. I've got to make that flight!"

At the airport the passengers were all on board as I helped carry my guests' bags to the plane. Bobby was the last to board. He turned as he stepped inside and gave me a wink,

"Marv, I've had a wonderful time. Lot's of fun.

I knew it would be. Anytime you want me back, anytime. You just call."

And he was gone!

Bobby Riggs caricatured in 1973

EPILOGUE

After the world found Aspen and its four major ski areas in the 70's, the area of Aspen and the surrounding communities of Snowmass, Carbondale, Woody Creek and Basalt exploded with second homes for the rich and famous. By 2007, the permanent population of 3,000 in the 70's has grown to 6,000, but the property values have skyrocketed. Prince Bandar of Saudi Arabia recently listed his Aspen property, a 56,000 square foot chalet for $135,000,000! Yes, $135 million! Aspen is probably one of the highest per square foot real estate markets in the world. Celebrities with homes in the Aspen area include Kevin Costner, Michael Douglas, Michael Eisner, Robert Wagner, Jill St. John and so on. Our project, the Aspen Club, has been sold several times over and is now The Aspen Club and Spa, a very posh private facility catering to health- oriented clients from around the world.

In 1985, even at the ripe old age of 67 and still as an active promoter and personal hustler of tennis, Riggs took another go at the spotlight by challenging the top women's doubles team of Pam Shriver and Martina Navratilova to still another "Battle of the Sexes", playing with former champion Vitas Gerulitis. Once again the women triumphed, in score, but who really knows who won the big money. Even the legendary tennis great Don Budge, who with Riggs, Jack Kramer, Pancho Gonzales and Fred Perry formed the first professional circuit and traveled together in the 40's, always suspected that with 8-5 odds to beat Billie Jean King, somehow Bobby had to have bet some big bucks on her to win. But no one will ever know.

Then in 1988, at the age of 70, and long out of the tennis spotlight, Bobby Riggs was diagnosed with prostate cancer. Realizing that the world knew little of this disease, Riggs chose to go public and share his diagnosis with the world and spoke wherever he could get an audience. In 1994 he set up the Bobby Riggs Museum Foundation to promote and fund prostate cancer awareness. He would spend the last year of his life educating men and women about the disease.

Washington Post, October 27, 1995 – "Bobby Riggs, 77, a former Wimbledon and U.S. Open tennis Champion who helped make women's tennis a major spectator and money sport by losing a widely promoted 1973 match to Billie Jean King, died of prostate cancer at his home in Leucadia, California. He was married and divorced twice and is survived by five children."

Now, you might be able to understand how I've come to the conclusion that Bobby Riggs was the greatest tennis players of all time. Hopefully Federer will someday make that kind of difference!

"And that's my Bobby Riggs' story."

Not to be left without the last word, Jay Paul informs me that one of his closest friends was one of the last people to speak with Riggs just before his passing. He asked him about the match with Billie Jean, whether he had thrown it or not. Bobby smiled and said, "I won!" and he was gone.

I've come to regard Bobby Riggs as even greater than great. I believe now that he never lost a match unless he wanted to. My hat goes off to him.